CITY SEC...

CHEYENNE MOUNTAIN COMPLEX

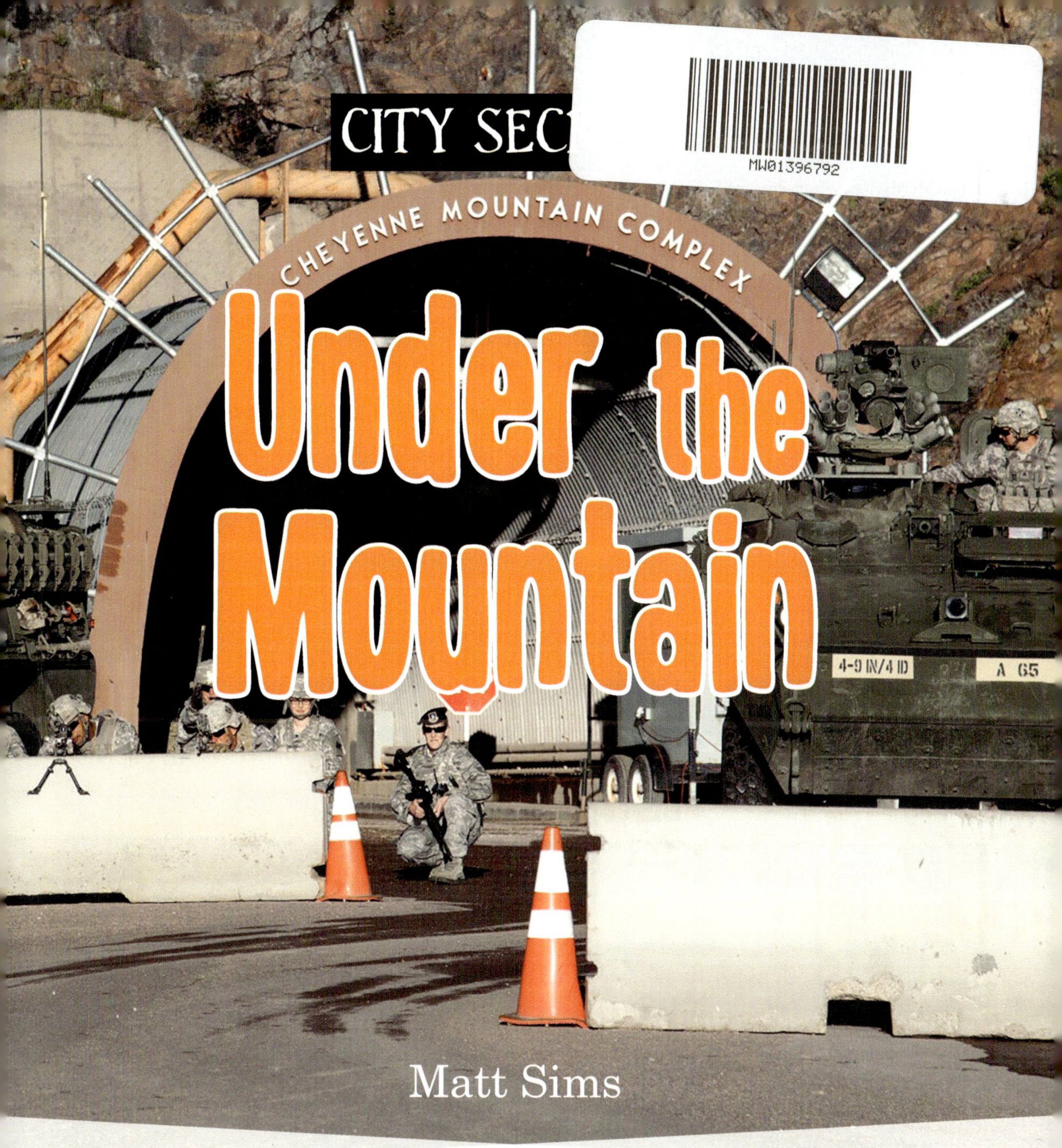

Under the Mountain

Matt Sims

high noon books

City Secrets: *Under the Mountain*
Sound Out Level 6

Each book in the Sound Out series is written in chapter format and gives students continued opportunities to practice decoding skills. Level 6 focuses on one-syllable spelling patterns, word endings, compound words, prefixes and suffixes, and simple two-syllable words.

Editor: Deb Akers
Book Design: Book Buddy Media

High Noon Books
a division of Academic Therapy Publications
20 Leveroni Court
Novato, CA 94949

Copyright 2009, 2018 by High Noon Books. All rights reserved. Printed in the United States of America. No part of this publication may be reproduced, stored in a retrieval system, or transmitted, in any form or by any means, electronic, mechanical photocopying, recording or otherwise, without the prior written permission of the publisher.

Images sourced from—
U.S. Air Force: cover (jet), pp. 1, 15; Wikimedia/Public Domain: cover (background), pp. 7, 8, 12, 13, 14, 16, 24, 29, 30; Getty Images: pp. 4, 5, 10, 18, 20, 21, 27; Newscom/ZUMA Press/Mark Richards: pp. 22, 28; Newscom/KRT: p. 25; Pixabay: background

International Standard Book Number: 978-1-63402-232-3

29 28 27 26 25 24 23 22 21
13 12 11 10 09 08 07 06 05

HighNoonBooks.com

Set Order #2234-7

Contents

NORAD 5

Blasting In 11

The Cold War 15

Life Inside 21

Secrets of NORAD 25

Stand Down 29

UNITED STATES OF AMERICA
Colorado
Denver

DENVER
AURORA
LAKEWOOD
GOLDEN
LITTLETON
PARKER
CASTLE ROCK
WOODMOOR
WOODLAND PARK
BLACK FOREST
COLORADO SPRINGS
NORAD
FOUNTAIN
PUEBLO
CANON CITY
PENROSE
GREENWOOD
TEXAS CREEK
MCCOY
GLENWOOD SPRINGS
GYPSUM
EDWARDS
VAIL
SILVERTHORNE
BRECKENRIDGE
CARBONDALE
BAILEY
LEADVILLE
FAIRPLAY
REDSTONE
ASPEN
TWIN LAKES
CRESTED BUTTE
BUENA VISTA
CRAFORD
GUNNISON
PONCHA SPRINGS
SALIDA
POWDERHORN
BYERS
LAST CHANCE
ANTON
AGATE
LIMON
HUGO
SIMLA
AROYA
PUNKIN CENTER
HASWELL
ORDWAY
70
25
24
285
50
36
40

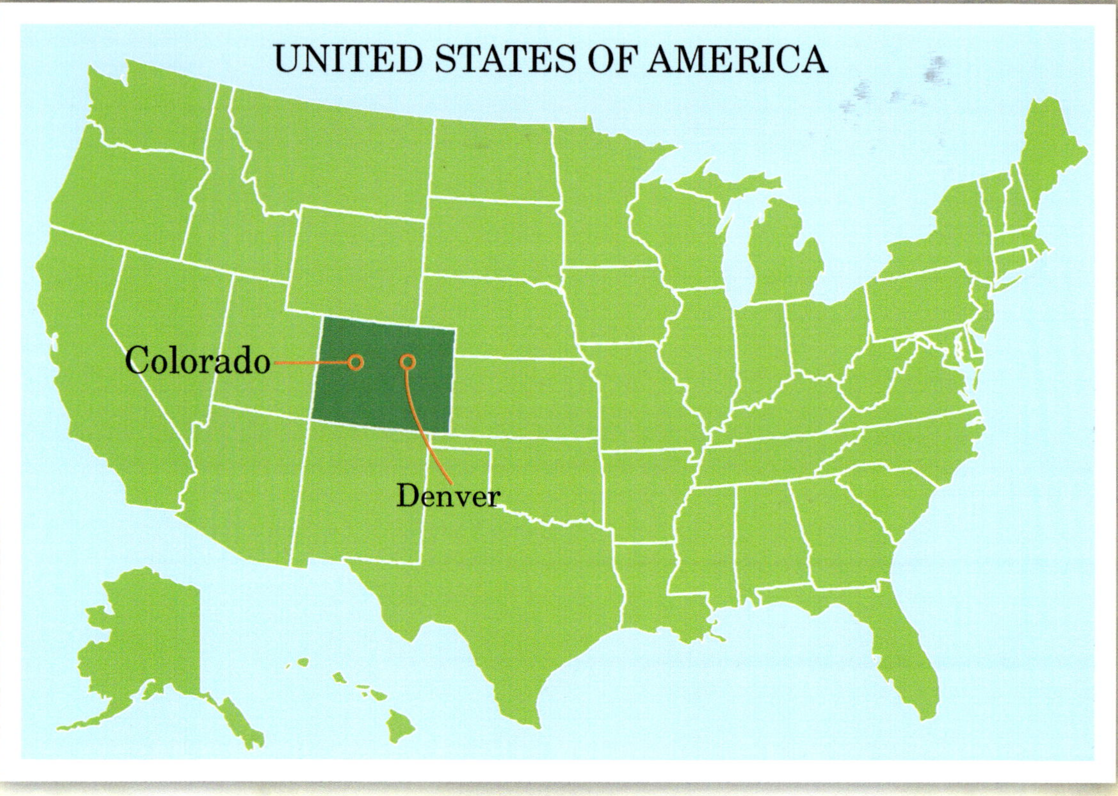

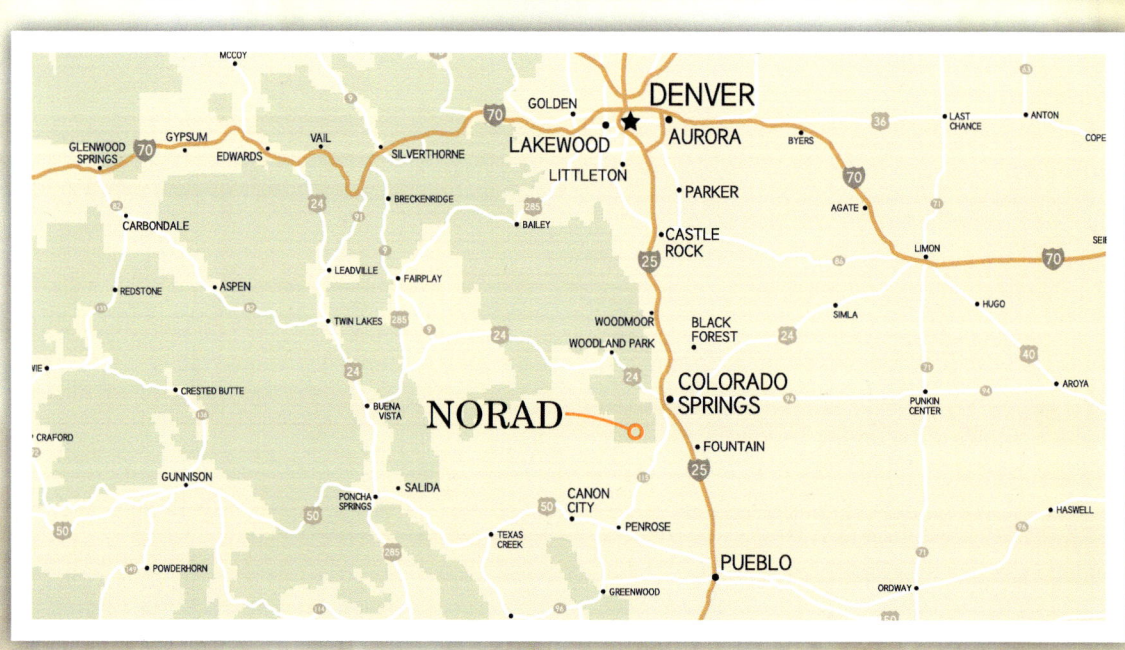

NORAD

The mountain peak turns red as the sun sets. The place looks peaceful. A hawk circles in the sky.

A car heads up the mountain. It drives along a narrow road. Are the people in the car going for a hike?

The NORAD base was in the mountains of Colorado.

The car slows down at the end of the road. It has come to a tunnel. There is a checkpoint by the side of the road. An arm comes out of the car window. A hand slips a card into a slot. The car drives into the tunnel.

Where does that tunnel go? It leads to a secret base called NORAD. The base is deep inside the mountain!

The NORAD base was built in the 1960s. Its job was to keep track of all plane flights over the U.S. and Canada. The staff at NORAD also used radar to watch for missiles that might be

NORAD staff watched all plane flights in the U.S. and Canada.

aimed at the U.S. They could send out warnings. They could help the country get ready for an attack.

No one could go inside the mountain

Cheyenne Mountain NORAD entrance, 1968

without a pass. This NORAD base has always been a top-secret place.

Why build a base inside a mountain? And how was it done? The answers might surprise you.

Workers blasted the rock away.

Blasting In

The workers set the first charge. Then they sat back. Boom! They watched the rocks explode. Rocks and pebbles flew up. The sky filled with clouds of dust.

The workers blasted into the mountain. They did it bit by bit. They were going to make a space deep inside. It would sit under 2,000 feet of rock.

The space would be about 100 feet tall. There would be room for office buildings. There would be tunnels that ran from place to place.

Tunnels were blasted out of the rock.

Miles of wire were put under the mountain. These would give the base power. Phone lines were put in. Big cables would link NORAD to the world. Now they could send out warnings if they saw danger.

People would be living and working inside the mountain. Air vents had to be built. They also had to put water pipes into the base. They made sure that NORAD was safe for the people inside.

Pipes brought in water and power.

NORAD's logo showed that the U.S. and Canada were working to keep the land, air, and sea safe.

The Cold War

The NORAD base cost a lot of money. It was very hard to build. Why did people spend all that time and money?

One of the entrances to the base

NORAD also watched Russian satellites.

The base was built during a scary time. It was called the Cold War. The U.S. was afraid it would be attacked. People thought an attack could happen at any time.

Russia (RUH-shuh) had atom bombs. It could use missiles to drop them on the U.S. The U.S. had atom bombs, too. It could use missiles to drop them on Russia. Each atom bomb could kill people for miles around.

The U.S. thought it could stay safe from the big bombs. NORAD could give people a warning. Then they could hide in their basements. They would wait until it was safe to come out again.

Later, people learned that the bombs were much worse than they had thought. These bombs could end human life. No

An atom bomb explodes.

one could hide from them.

NORAD did a lot to help the U.S. The base under the mountain helped keep the U.S. safe. But the U.S. did more than run NORAD. The U.S. also worked with Canada and other countries. This was a way to make the world safe. This is still true today.

People worked all day and all night at the base.

Life Inside

Not many people know what the NORAD base looked like. There are very few pictures of the inside of the base.

Inside the base

People walked through the tunnels to get to other buildings.

We do know that people lived and worked inside the mountain. We can make some guesses about life inside the NORAD base. There were rooms for people to sleep in. There were places to eat. There were places for the staff to relax after work.

We know that people walked through tunnels from place to place. There were even little trains that people rode. It would be fun to tour the NORAD base. A few people are able to go on tours. They have to know someone who works there.

People in the "war room" watched air traffic on their screens.

Secrets of NORAD

We have pictures of the "war room" in the NORAD base. That was a room full of big screens. The screens showed all the airplanes flying over the U.S. and Canada.

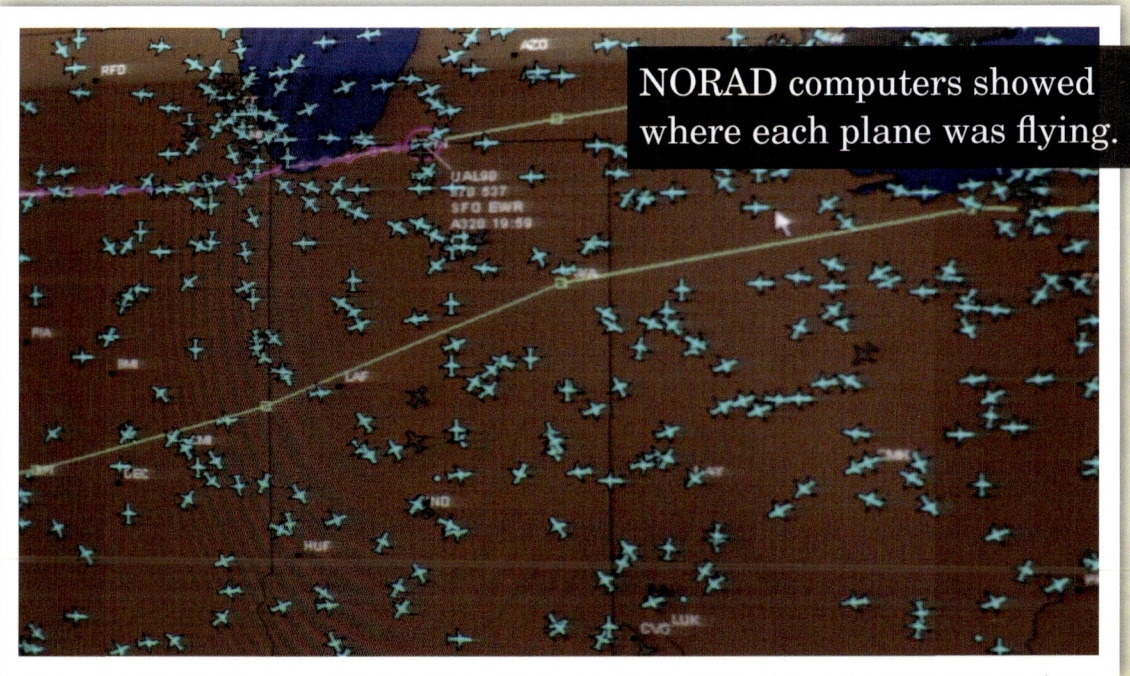

NORAD computers showed where each plane was flying.

The NORAD staff sat and watched the screens.

They looked for planes that did not belong there. They found out about any strange planes they saw.

No one got in or out of this room without a pass. The work done in this room was top secret. Very few people in the U.S. knew what went on in the "war room."

The command post of NORAD

Thick blast doors could block the shock wave from a bomb blast.

Stand Down

The NORAD base has huge doors. They are three feet thick. They were made to keep out a big bomb blast.

Open blast doors

In 1987, Russia and the U.S. signed a deal. The deal said how many missiles they would keep. After that, big bombs were less of a danger. There was less need for NORAD.

U.S. President Reagan and Russian President Gorbachev signed a deal in 1987.

In 2006, the NORAD base was told to "stand down." This means that it was partly closed.

Then NORAD moved to an Air Force base. It changed how it watched for planes and missiles.

Now the base is used just for training. It is also a "back-up" base. It would be used if other bases were not working.

High Frequency Words

a	go(ing)	out
all	has	over
an	have	that
as	help	the
at	in	there
be	into	they
by	is	to
come	it	up
does	look(s)	was
down	no	where
for	of	yes
get	or	